Miraculous Magic Tricks

CARD MAGIC

by Mike Lane

Illustrations by David Mostyn

WINDMILL
BOOKS ™

New York

Published in 2012 by Windmill Books, an Imprint of Rosen Publishing
29 East 21st Street, New York, NY 10010

First Edition

Author: Mike Lane
Editors: Patience Coster and Joe Harris
Illustrations: David Mostyn
Design: Tokiko Morishima

Library of Congress Cataloging-in-Publication Data

Lane, Mike.
 Card magic / by Mike Lane.
    p. cm.— (Miraculous magic tricks)
 Includes index.
 ISBN 978-1-61533-512-1 (library binding) — ISBN 978-1-
4488-6731-8 (pbk.) — ISBN 978-1-4488-6732-5 (6-pack)
 1. Card tricks. I. Title.
 GV1549.L36 2012
 793.85—dc23
                           2011025936
Printed in China

CPSIA Compliance Information: Batch # AW2102WM: For further information
contact Windmill Books, New York, New York at 1-866-478-0556

SL002047US

CONTENTS

INTRODUCTION

Within these pages you will discover great card tricks that are easy to do and impressive to watch.

To be a successful magician, you will need to practice the tricks in private before you perform them in front of an audience. An excellent way to practice is in front of a mirror, since you can watch the magic happen before your own eyes.

When performing, you must speak clearly, slowly, and loudly enough for everyone to hear. But never tell the audience what's going to happen.

Remember to "watch your angles." This means being careful about where your spectators are standing or sitting when you are performing. The best place is directly in front of you.

Never tell the secret of how the trick is done. If someone asks, just say: "It's magic!"

THE MAGICIAN'S PLEDGE

I promise not to reveal the secrets of magic to those who are not magicians.

I promise to practice these magic tricks over and over again before attempting to perform them in front of an audience.

I promise to respect my art, the art of magic.

MAGIC PLATE PREDICTION

ILLUSION
The spectator picks a card from the deck. The value of the card appears in a plate of soil held by the magician.

1 Before performing the trick, the magician chooses a card and places it in the deck second from the top.

2 Using the corner of a bar of soap, the magician writes the card value on a paper plate. For example, if the card is the four of hearts, he writes 4H.

3 The magician pours a little soil onto the plate, just enough to cover the base.

4 The magician places the deck face down. Now he is ready to begin the trick.

5 He cuts the deck in half and places the two halves side by side.

6 He takes the first card from the pile that was the top half of the deck, and places it on the bottom half.

7 The magician points to the next card in the pile (which is the card he previously prepared) and asks the spectator to take it, look at it, and hold on to it.

8 The magician slowly swirls the soil around in the plate. The value of the card in the spectator's hand is revealed. The magician asks the spectator to show his card to confirm that it is indeed the same.

JUMPING JACKS

1 The magician holds up four jacks from a deck of cards, with the faces of the cards toward the spectator. The cards should overlap one another in a fan-like manner.

2 The magician has hidden four random cards behind the jacks. He holds these at the back with his thumb, while using his fingers to hold the cards at the front.

9

3 Using both hands, the magician pushes the four jacks together, keeping the random cards behind them.

4 The magician now places the eight cards (the spectator believes there are just four jacks) face down on top of the deck.

I WILL PLACE THIS JACK SOMEWHERE IN THE DECK.

5 Next the magician removes the first card (which is a random card) from the deck, saying: "I will place this jack somewhere in the deck." He slides the card into the deck, being careful not to show its face and give the game away!

6 He does exactly the same with the next three cards.

7 The magician now waves his hand dramatically over the deck.

8 He turns over the top four cards to show that the jacks have jumped back from the middle of the deck to the top!

PICKPOCKET

ILLUSION

The magician asks the spectator to choose a card from the deck. The spectator returns the card to the deck without showing it to the magician. The spectator now shuffles the deck. The magician puts the deck in his pocket. He then reaches into his pocket and pulls out the spectator's card.

1 Prior to the trick, the magician picks a card and places it in the deck second from the top.

2 The magician places a duplicate of this card in his pocket.

3 He now begins the trick with the deck of cards face down.

4 The magician cuts the deck (or asks the spectator to do so) and places the two halves side by side. It is important that the magician remembers which is the top half of the deck.

5 The magician takes the top card off the top half and places it on the other half.

6 The magician points to the next card in the pile. This is the card of which he has the duplicate. He asks the spectator to take this card, look at it, and remember it.

7 He then asks the spectator to shuffle the card back into the deck.

DUPLICATE CARD

8 The magician now puts the deck in his pocket, being careful to place it behind the duplicate card.

9 The magician moves his hand around in his pocket, as if searching for the spectator's card. Much to everyone's amazement, he pulls out the spectator's (the duplicate) card!

TAP TO TOP

ILLUSION

The magician shows the spectator the top card of a deck and then places the card in the middle of the deck. He taps the deck. Hey presto—the card is back on top!

DOUBLE LIFT

1 The magician starts by picking up the top two cards together. He does this by holding them by opposite corners and bending them slightly to create the appearance of one card (this is called a double lift).

2 The magician shows the face of the card(s) to the spectator. He is in fact showing the face of the bottom card.

15

3 The magician replaces the cards on top of the deck.

4 The magician takes the top card off the deck and inserts it in the middle, without showing its face.

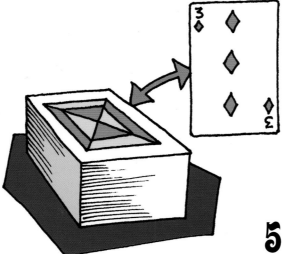

5 The card left on top of the deck is the card the spectator saw.

6 The magician taps the deck dramatically three times.

7 He turns over the top card to reveal that the card the spectator chose has jumped up from the middle of the deck!

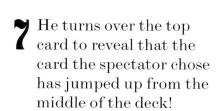

BALANCING ACT

1 Prior to the trick, the magician applies a small amount of wax, petroleum jelly, or lip balm to his fingertip.

2 The magician asks the spectator to choose two cards from a deck.

3 The magician asks the spectator to keep one card and give the other card to him (the spectator is allowed to choose which card he wants).

4 The magician holds his index finger straight up in the air while keeping his other fingers curled in. He asks the spectator to do the same.

5 Holding the card horizontally, the magician places it centrally on his index finger while steadying it with his other hand. He asks the spectator to do the same.

6 The magician lets go of the card and it remains balanced on his index finger.

7 When the spectator tries to do the same, he can't get the card to balance!

A RISING CARD

ILLUSION

The spectator chooses a card from the deck, replaces it, and watches in amazement as the card slowly rises from the middle of the deck.

1 Prior to the trick, the magician prepares the deck. Holding a card lengthwise, he places his thumb against the back of it.

2 He draws round his thumb with a marker.

3 With a pair of scissors, he cuts the card along the marker line. He needs to do this with a total of 23 cards. These are known as "gimmicked cards."

4 The magician stacks the gimmicked cards on top of one another.

5 He puts two ordinary cards face down on top of the gimmicked cards. He is now ready to perform.

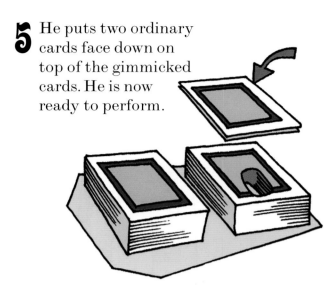

6 The magician starts by cutting the deck and placing the halves side by side. He hands the bottom half to the spectator, saying: "This is your half and this is mine." The magician keeps the half with the gimmicked cards.

7 The magician asks the spectator to look through his half, pick a card, and hold on to it.

8 He now asks the spectator to put the deck down and place his chosen card on top. The magician places his deck on top of the spectator's.

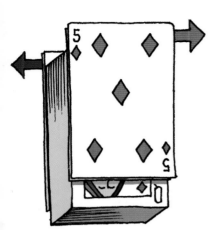

9 The magician picks up the entire deck, holding it so that the cards face the spectator. Declaring that he wants to make the deck a bit lighter, the magician removes two cards from the top and two from the bottom.

10 While doing this, the magician inserts his index finger into the bottom of the gimmicked cards and slowly pushes the spectator's card (the top card in the ungimmicked deck) so that it rises up above the other cards.

1 His action is hidden by the cards he is removing from the top and bottom of the deck. Pure magic!

PICK A CARD, FIND A CARD

1 The magician hands a deck
of cards to the spectator,
who is allowed to examine
and shuffle them.

2 The magician takes the deck
and quickly fans out the cards
face up, to confirm that they
are in no particular order.

3 While doing this, the magician
looks at and remembers the card
that will be the second from the
top. He then closes the deck and
places it face down on the table.

4 The magician splits the deck and places the two halves side by side. He must remember which is the top of the deck.

5 The magician then takes the top card from the top half of the deck and places it on the bottom half.

6 The magician points to the next card in the first pile (which is the card he remembered) and tells the spectator to look at it and remember it.

7 He tells the spectator to put the card back anywhere in the deck and to shuffle all the cards together.

8 The magician looks through the deck and easily picks out the card the spectator memorized, since he already knows what it is!

AN EVEN ODDER CARD TRICK

ILLUSION
The magician splits a deck of cards in half. The spectator chooses a card from one half and places it in the other half. A second spectator does the same with the other half. The magician easily finds the two cards.

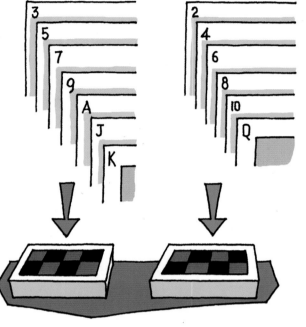

1 Prior to performing the trick, the magician prepares the deck. In one half he places all the odd numbered cards (3, 5, 7, etc.) together with the aces, jacks, and kings; in the other half he places all the even numbered cards (2, 4, 6, etc.) together with the queens. He places the two halves side by side. He is now ready to perform.

2 The magician gives the spectator one half and asks him to take a card, look at it, and place it in the other half.

3 The magician gives the other half to another spectator and asks him to take a card, look at it, and place it in the first half.

4 The magician now asks the spectators to shuffle each of the decks. (The halves are shuffled separately.)

5 The magician picks up the first half and looks through the cards. He just has to find the even card in a deck of odd numbers. He does the same with the second half, finding an odd numbered card in a deck of even numbers.

6 With a flourish, the magician shows the two cards to the spectators. How on earth did he do that?!

PLAYING CARD LINE-UP

ILLUSION

This trick is based on a mathematical concept. The magician places 21 cards face up in front of the spectator. He asks the spectator to memorize one of them. The magician is able to find the card the spectator has memorized.

1 The magician hands 21 cards to the spectator to examine and shuffle. The spectator then returns the cards to the magician.

2 Holding the cards in one hand, the magician turns them over one at a time. He lays the first three cards down from left to right, and then continues this pattern to create three columns of seven cards. The cards should overlap so only part of the face of each card is showing.

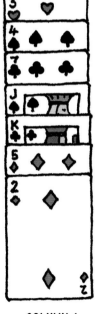

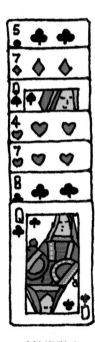

COLUMN 1   **COLUMN 2**   **COLUMN 3**

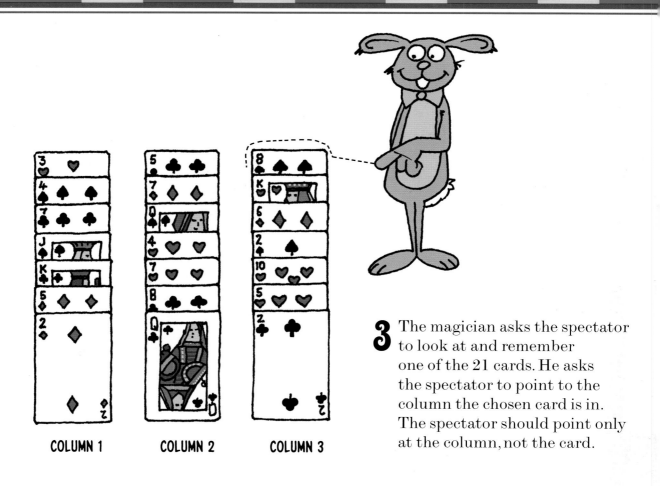

COLUMN 1 COLUMN 2 COLUMN 3

3 The magician asks the spectator to look at and remember one of the 21 cards. He asks the spectator to point to the column the chosen card is in. The spectator should point only at the column, not the card.

4 The magician now picks up each column, keeping the cards in the same order. He makes a pile, placing the column with the spectator's card in the middle, sandwiched between the other two columns.

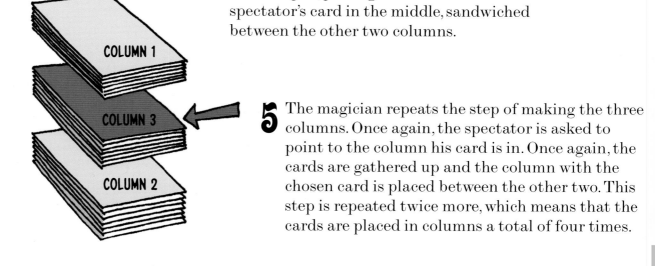

COLUMN 1

COLUMN 3

COLUMN 2

5 The magician repeats the step of making the three columns. Once again, the spectator is asked to point to the column his card is in. Once again, the cards are gathered up and the column with the chosen card is placed between the other two. This step is repeated twice more, which means that the cards are placed in columns a total of four times.

6 When the cards are placed down the fourth and final time, the magician does not ask the spectator to choose one. This time, the magician points to the middle row and states that the spectator's card is in that row. The magician now points to the fourth card in the middle row. This will be the spectator's card!

7 Another ending for this trick is as follows: after picking up the piles for the third time, the magician tells the spectator that the chosen card will be the eleventh card that is turned over from the top. And, magically, it is!

FURTHER READING

Barnhart, Norm. *Amazing Magic Tricks.* Mankato, MN: Capstone Press, 2008.

Cassidy, John and Michael Stroud. *Klutz Book of Magic.* Palo Alto, CA: Klutz Press, 2006.

Charney, Steve. *Cool Card Tricks.* Mankato, MN: Capstone Press, 2011.

Klingel, Cynthia. *Card Tricks.* Mankato, MN: Compass Point Books, 2002.

Longe, Bob. *Little Giant Book of Card Tricks.* New York: Sterling Publishers Inc, 2000.

WEB SITES

For Web resources related to the subject of this book, go to: www.windmillbooks.com/weblinks and select this book's title.

GLOSSARY

double lift (DUH-bul LIFT) Two cards made to look like one.

duplicate (DOO-plih-ket) A second card exactly the same as the first.

gimmicked (GIH-mikd) A card Altered or marked in some way.

index finger (IN-deks FIN-gur) The finger next to the thumb.

memorize (MEH-muh-ryz) To learn by heart.

ungimmicked (un-GIH-mikd) Unmarked or unaltered.

INDEX